Montana T Guide 2025

Uncover the Top Spots in the Treasure State: Visit Stunning National Parks, Hidden Gems, Exciting Outdoor Adventures, and Delicious Local Eats

Michael J. Ashley

No part of this book may be reproduced in any form or by any electronic or mechanical mean, including information storage and retrieval systems, without permission in writing from the publisher, except by the reviewer who may quote brief passage in a review. This book is a work of non-fiction. The views and opinions expressed in this book are the author's own and do not necessarily reflect those of the publisher or any other person or organization. The information in this book is provided for education and informational purposes only. It is not intended as a substitute for professional advice of any kind.

Copyright 2025 © Michael J. Ashley All right reserved.

Table of content

- Table of content... 3
- General map of Montana.. 6
- CHAPTER 1..7
- INTRODUCTION..7
  - Welcome to Montana - The Treasure State....... 7
  - Why Visit Montana?... 8
  - What Makes Montana Unique............................9
  - How This Guide Will Help You..........................11
- CHAPTER 2...13
- Planning Your Trip... 13
  - Best Time to Visit Montana............................. 13
  - How to Get There...15
  - Entry Requirements and Travel Tips................17
  - Getting Around Montana (Public Transport, Car Rentals, and More)..19
  - Packing Essentials for Your Montana Adventure 21
- CHAPTER 3...26
- Top Attractions & Must-Sees.............................. 26
  - Glacier National Park: Nature's Masterpiece.. 26
  - Yellowstone National Park: The First National Park..29
  - Big Sky Resort: Skiing and Outdoor Adventures 32
  - The National Bison Range: Wildlife Encounters. 35
  - The Museum of the Rockies: A Journey Through Time..37
- CHAPTER 4...41

The Beartooth Highway: Scenic Drives & Road Trips.. 41
  Flathead Lake: Peaceful Escape.................... 43
  Crystal Park: Gemstone Hunting......................46
  Local Festivals and Traditions.........................48
CHAPTER 5...**51**
Outdoor Adventures..**51**
  Hiking and Trekking: Trails in Glacier & Yellowstone.. 51
  Wildlife Safaris and Birdwatching in Montana. 53
  Water Activities: Kayaking, Boating, and Fishing 55
  Winter Sports: Skiing, Snowboarding, and Snowshoeing...57
  Scenic Drives: Exploring Montana's Natural Beauty.. 58
Chapter 6.. **61**
Food and Drink..**61**
  Classic Montana Cuisine: Steaks, Bison, and More.. 61
  Best Places to Eat in Montana: From Fine Dining to Local Delights.................................... 65
  Craft Breweries and Distilleries....................... 69
CHAPTER 7...**73**
Accommodation Options................................... **73**
  Luxury Hotels and Resorts in Montana........... 73
  Mid-Range Stays: Comfortable and Convenient. 77
  Budget-Friendly Lodging: Motels, Hostels, and Campsites... 80
  Unique Accommodations: Dude Ranches,

Cabins, and Glamping..................................83
CHAPTER 8..**86**
Day Trips and Excursions................................. **86**
   Day Trips from Billings, Missoula, and Bozeman 87
   Flathead Valley and the Mission Mountains....89
   Exploring the Bitterroot Valley..........................92
CHAPTER 9..**95**
Health and Safety Tips....................................... **95**
   Health and Safety Tips for Your Montana Adventure..96
   Dealing with Wildlife Encounters.....................98
   First Aid & Emergency Services in Montana.100
CHAPTER 10..**102**
Bonus Section...**102**
   Itineraries.. 102
      Final Thoughts... 108
CONCLUSION..**108**

General map of Montana

Scan with device to view map

CHAPTER 1

INTRODUCTION

Welcome to Montana - The Treasure State

Montana, located in the northwestern U.S., is a place of stunning landscapes, towering mountains, and crystal-clear lakes. Known as the "Treasure State," it offers both rugged wilderness and warm, welcoming communities. Whether you're looking for adventure or relaxation, Montana has something for everyone.

This guide is your key to exploring Montana's vast outdoor activities, iconic parks like Yellowstone and Glacier National Park, and charming small towns. You'll also discover the local food, drink, and rich culture that make Montana special.

Montana's wild landscapes provide endless adventure, from hiking and skiing to spotting wildlife. But its fascinating history, including Old

West landmarks and Native American heritage, is just as captivating. Along with outdoor thrills, you'll enjoy hearty steaks, craft beers, and delicious local cuisine.

Beyond famous parks, Montana has hidden gems, from peaceful lakesides to quiet wilderness. You'll find unspoiled spots that offer a true connection to nature.

Safety is important, and this guide provides tips on staying healthy, protecting yourself from the elements, and handling wildlife encounters.

No matter your reason for visiting, Montana will leave you with unforgettable memories. This book will help you explore with confidence, whether it's your first trip or you're returning for more adventures. Welcome to Montana, where adventure, beauty, and history await!

Why Visit Montana?

Montana is known for its wide-open spaces and outdoor activities, but there's much more to discover. The state's natural beauty and unique history draw visitors from all over.

Montana offers breathtaking landscapes, perfect for hiking, fishing, skiing, and wildlife watching.

Famous spots like Glacier and Yellowstone National Parks showcase Montana's stunning nature, where you can find adventure and wonder at every turn.

Montana's history is just as rich. From the Old West to Native American heritage, Montana is filled with historic sites, ghost towns, and landmarks. You can explore the Lewis and Clark Trail or learn about the state's mining past.

The people of Montana are also a highlight. Small towns like Bozeman, Missoula, and Billings offer modern amenities in a laid-back, welcoming atmosphere. The locals take pride in their heritage and love sharing their stories with visitors.

What Makes Montana Unique

Montana's uniqueness comes from its natural beauty, rich history, and distinct local culture. Known as "Big Sky Country," Montana offers wide-open views and stunning sunsets that make it feel unlike anywhere else. The vast landscapes are

peaceful, offering a chance to reflect and enjoy nature.

Montana is steeped in history, from the Lewis and Clark Expedition to Native American heritage. You

can visit landmarks that tell the story of the land, its people, and their challenges.

The state is diverse, with everything from rugged mountains to wide plains. Whether you're kayaking, hiking, or spotting wildlife, Montana's varied terrain offers endless opportunities for adventure.

The state's remote beauty makes it ideal for those seeking peace or excitement.

Montana's people are another key element that sets the state apart. The locals are known for their kindness and hospitality, making visitors feel at home. Whether in big cities or small towns, you'll find friendly faces and a strong sense of pride in Montana's history. It's the combination of beauty, history, and warmth that makes Montana truly special.

How This Guide Will Help You

This guide is here to help you make the most of your time in Montana. It includes practical information, helpful tips, and recommendations for exploring Montana's stunning landscapes and cultural attractions.

In this book, you'll find the best outdoor activities, from hiking in Glacier National Park to visiting the geothermal wonders of Yellowstone. You'll also

discover hidden gems, including peaceful lakes and charming towns. We'll show you where to find the best food, including local dishes and craft beverages.

You'll also get advice on staying safe, finding accommodations, and traveling around Montana.

This guide will provide all the essentials, from when to visit to local customs.

With this guide, you'll have everything you need to enjoy Montana's beauty, culture, and adventure. Your journey starts here!

CHAPTER 2

Planning Your Trip

Best Time to Visit Montana

The best time to visit Montana really depends on what kind of experience you want. The state has something special to offer in every season, so no matter when you visit, you're bound to have a great time.

Summer (June to August): Summer is perfect for anyone who loves the outdoors. With temperatures ranging from 70°F to 85°F, it's a great time to hike, fish, and explore famous parks like Glacier and Yellowstone. The summer also brings beautiful wildflowers and cooler evenings, making it ideal for camping. This is also the season for popular festivals and outdoor concerts, such as the Sweet Pea Festival in Bozeman and the Montana Folk Festival in Butte.

Fall (September to November): Fall is the best time to visit if you're looking for a quieter, more peaceful experience. The weather cools down with temperatures between 50°F and 70°F, and the leaves turn vibrant red, orange, and yellow. Fall is also a great time to see wildlife, like elk and deer, as they prepare for winter. Fewer tourists visit during this season, and the drives along scenic roads like the Beartooth Highway are breathtaking. It's also hunting season, which is popular in Montana.

Winter (December to February): If you enjoy winter sports, Montana in winter is a dream. The snow-covered mountains offer some of the best skiing and snowboarding in the U.S., with resorts like Big Sky, Whitefish Mountain, and Bridger Bowl. The temperatures can drop below freezing, but the snowy scenery is well worth it. Winter also offers snowshoeing, ice fishing, and even dog sledding.

Spring (March to May): Spring is a time of renewal in Montana. While the temperatures range from 30°F to 60°F, the snow starts to melt, revealing the lush green landscape. It's a great time for hiking and wildlife watching as animals come out of hibernation. Spring is also quieter, making it an ideal time to visit before the summer crowds arrive.

Each season offers something unique, so the best time to visit depends on what kind of activities and experiences you're looking for. Whether you love the summer sun, the winter snow, or the beauty of autumn, Montana has something for you all year round.

How to Get There

There are several ways to get to Montana, depending on where you're coming from and how you prefer to travel. Here's what you need to know:

By Air: Montana has several airports, with the largest ones in Billings (Billings Logan International Airport), Bozeman (Bozeman Yellowstone International Airport), and Missoula (Missoula International Airport). These airports have direct flights from big U.S. cities like Denver, Seattle, Salt Lake City, and Minneapolis. You can easily rent a car at these airports to explore the rest of the state. Smaller regional airports are also available in cities like Kalispell, Great Falls, and Helena, making Montana's more remote areas easy to access.

By Car: Driving is one of the best ways to explore Montana since the state is vast and offers plenty of scenic routes. The highways are well-maintained, and road trips are a popular way to take in the beautiful landscapes. Interstate highways like I-90 and I-15 connect Montana to nearby states like Wyoming, Idaho, and North Dakota, making it easy to reach by car, especially if you're coming from the Pacific Northwest, the Midwest, or the Rockies.

By Train: Amtrak offers train routes through Montana, including the Empire Builder and California Zephyr, which connect the state to cities like Chicago and Seattle. Train travel may not be as common as flying or driving, but it can be a relaxing and scenic way to travel, especially from northern or western U.S. cities.

By Bus: Bus travel, though less common for tourists, is another budget-friendly way to get to Montana. Greyhound and other bus services run routes into cities like Billings, Missoula, and Bozeman. Once in Montana, bus connections to other parts of the state are available, though they are more limited compared to car or air travel.

Entry Requirements and Travel Tips

Montana is a welcoming place, and getting in is easy depending on where you're coming from. Here's what you need to know:

For U.S. Citizens: If you're traveling from within the United States, you don't need anything special to enter Montana. Just bring a valid ID, like a driver's license or state-issued ID, especially if you're flying. Minors may need a birth certificate or passport for air travel.

For International Travelers: If you're coming from outside the U.S., you'll need a valid passport. Depending on your home country, you may also need a visa. Most visitors from countries under the U.S. Visa Waiver Program (VWP) can travel without a visa for up to 90 days. It's always a good idea to check the U.S. State Department's website for the most current travel and visa rules.

Travel Insurance: While it's not required, travel insurance is a good idea for anyone planning adventurous activities like hiking, skiing, or rafting. Insurance can cover unexpected issues like trip cancellations, lost luggage, or medical emergencies.

Health and Safety Tips: Montana's wild landscape is beautiful, but it can also present challenges. If you're hiking or exploring remote areas, be aware of risks like wildlife encounters, extreme weather, and high altitudes. Always carry a basic first-aid kit, enough water, and proper clothing for the weather. In more isolated areas, cell phone service may be limited, so it's wise to tell someone your plans if you're heading into the wilderness.

Packing Tips: When packing for Montana, it's important to be prepared for all types of weather. The weather can change quickly, especially in the mountains, so pack layers. Include light, moisture-wicking clothing for outdoor activities, warm layers for cool evenings, and waterproof items in case of rain. Don't forget comfortable hiking boots if you plan to hit the trails, and a good camera to capture the amazing views.

With some preparation and these tips in mind, your trip to Montana will be smooth and enjoyable, no matter when you visit or how you travel.

Getting Around Montana (Public Transport, Car Rentals, and More)

Since Montana is a large state with remote areas, getting around is an important part of your travel plans. While public transportation options aren't as extensive as in big cities, there are still several ways to explore the state based on your preferences.

By Car: Driving is the most popular and flexible way to travel around Montana. With its open roads and stunning scenery, a road trip through the state is an unforgettable experience. Major highways like I-90 and I-15 connect you to important cities and neighboring states, while scenic routes like Beartooth Highway and Going-to-the-Sun Road in Glacier National Park offer beautiful views that make every mile special. Car rentals are available at major airports like Billings, Bozeman, Missoula, and Kalispell, as well as in smaller towns. Renting a car is usually the best option if you want to explore Montana's more remote areas.

Public Transportation: Montana doesn't have a full public transportation system, but there are some options, especially in larger cities like Billings, Bozeman, and Missoula, where city buses can take you around. For travel between cities and rural areas, options are limited. Greyhound and other bus services run routes between major cities, but these may be less frequent and don't cover more remote areas. Amtrak trains also pass through Montana, including the Empire Builder route to cities like Chicago and Seattle. While trains are not as commonly used as cars, they can be a relaxing and scenic way to see the state.

Taxis and Ride-Sharing: In larger cities, you can find taxis and use ride-sharing services like Uber and Lyft for short trips. However, in smaller towns or rural areas, these services may not be available, so it's a good idea to check ahead and plan your transport accordingly.

Biking: Montana offers beautiful biking trails for those who want a more active way to get around. Cities like Missoula and Bozeman are bike-friendly, and there are several cycling routes across the state that take you through scenic landscapes. Renting a bike for a few days is a great way to explore parks and smaller towns.

Guided Tours: If you'd rather not worry about transportation and want a more relaxed way to see the state, consider joining a guided tour. Many local companies offer tours, including wildlife safaris and hikes through national parks. These tours often include transportation, so you can just sit back and enjoy the sights while experts take care of the planning.

Packing Essentials for Your Montana Adventure

Packing for Montana can be tricky, as the weather can change quickly depending on the season, location, and altitude. Here's a list of things you should bring to make sure you're ready for whatever comes your way:

Layered Clothing: The weather in Montana can be unpredictable, so it's important to pack clothes that you can layer. Bring moisture-wicking base layers, fleece or lightweight jackets for warmth, and waterproof outer layers in case of rain or snow. In the mountains, temperatures can drop even during summer, so layering is key to staying comfortable.

Sturdy Hiking Boots: If you plan to hike, you'll need good-quality hiking boots. Montana has many trails, and you'll likely encounter rough, uneven terrain. Make sure your boots are waterproof and comfortable for long walks, so you can enjoy the adventure without discomfort.

Daypack: A small, lightweight backpack is perfect for carrying essentials during day hikes or outdoor activities. It should be big enough to hold water, snacks, sunscreen, a first-aid kit, and your camera, but not so big that it feels cumbersome on shorter trips.

Sunscreen and Sunglasses: With Montana's wide-open skies and high altitudes, you're exposed to more sunlight than you might think. Even on cooler days, it's easy to get sunburned. Pack sunscreen with at least SPF 30 and sunglasses with UV protection to keep your skin and eyes safe.

Water Bottles: Staying hydrated is important, especially if you're spending a lot of time outdoors. Bring a refillable water bottle so you can drink water throughout the day. If you're heading to remote areas where water sources are scarce, it might be a good idea to bring a portable water filter or purification tablets in case you need to refill from streams or lakes.

Camera or Smartphone: Montana's natural beauty is extraordinary, so don't forget your camera or smartphone to capture the incredible views. Whether you're photographing mountains, lakes, or wildlife, you'll want to document your experience. A camera with a zoom lens is helpful for capturing animals from a safe distance.

Binoculars: If you're interested in wildlife watching, binoculars are a must. Montana is home to animals like elk, bison, grizzly bears, and eagles. A good pair of binoculars lets you get a closer look at these amazing creatures from afar.

Travel Insurance: Although it's not a packing item, travel insurance is a smart choice for peace of mind, especially if you're planning adventure activities like hiking, skiing, or rafting. It can cover unexpected issues like illness, cancellations, or lost luggage.

Emergency and First Aid Kit: Montana's remote areas may make it hard to get help quickly. It's a good idea to bring a basic first-aid kit with bandages, antiseptic, pain relievers, insect repellent, and any personal medications you need. Being prepared for minor injuries or illnesses can be a lifesaver when you're in the wilderness.

Portable Power Bank: If you're going into remote areas where you may not have access to power outlets, a portable power bank is a handy item. It will keep your phone or camera charged throughout the day, especially if you rely on it for navigation or emergency contact

By packing these essential items and preparing for different weather conditions, you'll be ready to enjoy everything Montana has to offer. Whether you're hiking through national parks, skiing down snowy slopes, or relaxing by a lake, these packing tips will help keep you comfortable and safe throughout your trip.

CHAPTER 3

Top Attractions & Must-Sees

Montana is a state brimming with breathtaking natural wonders, historical landmarks, and rich cultural experiences. From towering mountain ranges to expansive wildlife reserves, pristine lakes, and world-class museums, this state offers something for every kind of traveler. In this chapter, we'll dive into some of the most awe-inspiring places you should not miss. Whether you're looking for outdoor adventures, stunning landscapes, or a step back in time, Montana's top attractions promise unforgettable memories.

Glacier National Park: Nature's Masterpiece

Overview: Often referred to as the "Crown of the Continent," Glacier National Park is a gem of the northern Rocky Mountains. Spanning over 1 million acres, the park features majestic peaks, deep valleys, lush forests, and over 26 glaciers left over from the Ice Age. This park is an outdoor lover's dream, offering everything from serene lakes to

 rugged hiking trails, making it one of the most iconic natural attractions in North America.

What to See

Going-to-the-Sun Road: This 50-mile scenic byway is one of the park's most famous attractions. It offers stunning panoramic views as it weaves through glacial valleys, alpine meadows, and waterfalls. The road is also one of the few in the world that crosses the Continental Divide, providing spectacular vistas of the park's diverse landscapes.

Lake McDonald: This large, tranquil lake is surrounded by snow-capped mountains and dense forests. Its crystal-clear waters perfectly reflect the towering peaks, making it a peaceful spot for kayaking, boating, or simply relaxing. In winter, the lake transforms into a quiet, snow-covered wonder.

Hidden Lake Overlook: For a moderate hike with rewarding views, head to the Hidden Lake Overlook. The hike offers incredible vistas of Hidden Lake, nestled among the mountains, with wildflowers in full bloom during the summer months.

Wildlife: The park is home to a wide variety of wildlife, including grizzly bears, black bears, bighorn sheep, mountain goats, and wolves. Visitors often spot these magnificent creatures in their natural habitats, particularly during early mornings or at dusk.

Best Time to Visit

The best time to visit Glacier National Park is during the summer months, from June to

September, when the majority of the park's roads and hiking trails are open. However, winter is an equally magical time to visit for those interested in snowshoeing, skiing, or enjoying the tranquil beauty of the park without the crowds.

Yellowstone National Park: The First National Park

Overview

Yellowstone National Park, the first national park in the world, is a vast and varied landscape that spans three states—Wyoming, Montana, and Idaho. Established in 1872, Yellowstone is famous for its geothermal features, such as geysers and hot springs, as well as its abundant wildlife and striking scenery. The park is a must-see for nature lovers, history enthusiasts, and adventure seekers.

What to See

Old Faithful: Old Faithful is one of Yellowstone's most famous landmarks, known for its predictable eruptions, which happen about every 90 minutes. Watching this geyser shoot hot water and steam high into the air is one of the park's most iconic experiences.

Grand Prismatic Spring: The Grand Prismatic Spring is the largest hot spring in the U.S., known for its vivid blue, orange, and green colors caused by bacteria and minerals in the water. Its brilliant hues make it one of the most photographed sites in Yellowstone.

Yellowstone Lake: This large, tranquil lake is the heart of the park, surrounded by majestic mountains and lush forests. Visitors can enjoy boating, fishing, or hiking around the lake, and in winter, it becomes a beautiful, snow-covered destination.

Wildlife Watching: Yellowstone is home to an impressive array of wildlife, including bison, elk, wolves, and grizzly bears. The Lamar Valley and Hayden Valley are prime spots for wildlife sightings, especially during the early morning or late evening.

Norris Geyser Basin: Known for its extreme geothermal activity, the Norris Geyser Basin is home to boiling springs and the famous Steamboat Geyser, the tallest active geyser in the world. A walk through the area offers

a fascinating look at the raw power of nature.

Best Time to Visit

The best time to visit Yellowstone is during the warmer months, from June to September, when most of the park's roads and facilities are open. However, the fall season, when the crowds thin out and the foliage changes color, is also a beautiful time to experience the park.

Big Sky Resort: Skiing and Outdoor Adventures

Overview Big Sky Resort, located in southwestern Montana, is one of the largest ski areas in the United States.

With over 5,800 acres of skiable terrain, it's a haven for winter sports enthusiasts. But Big Sky isn't just a winter destination—it's also a year-round resort offering activities like mountain biking, hiking, and zip-lining, making it an all-season destination for adventure lovers.

What to Do

Skiing and Snowboarding: Big Sky boasts a wide variety of slopes for all skill levels, from beginner runs to challenging expert terrain. The resort also features terrain parks, tree runs, and vast open bowls. The ski season typically runs from November to April, giving you plenty of time to enjoy the snow.

Mountain Biking and Hiking: In the warmer months, Big Sky turns into a mountain biking and hiking paradise. The resort offers miles of trails that take you through stunning landscapes, providing excellent views of the surrounding mountains and valleys.

Zip Line and Scenic Gondola Rides: For those seeking thrills beyond skiing, Big Sky offers exciting zip line rides and scenic gondola trips that provide breathtaking views of the resort and Gallatin National Forest.

Après Ski: After a day on the slopes, unwind at one of the resort's après-ski spots, where you can enjoy hot drinks, local beers, and hearty meals. Big Sky also has luxurious accommodations and spas to help you relax and rejuvenate after a day of outdoor fun.

Best Time to Visit

Big Sky is a popular winter destination, with the best conditions for skiing and snowboarding between December and March. However, summer offers a great alternative for outdoor enthusiasts looking to enjoy biking, hiking, and scenic views

The National Bison Range: Wildlife Encounters

Overview: Located in northwestern Montana, the National Bison Range is a wildlife reserve dedicated to conserving bison and other native species. The range spans 18,500 acres and is home to a large herd of bison, as well as elk, deer, bighorn sheep, and a variety of bird species.

It's an excellent destination for wildlife watchers and anyone interested in experiencing Montana's natural beauty.

What to See

Bison Herds: The National Bison Range is famous for its large herd of bison. Visitors can watch these magnificent animals as they roam freely across the plains. The sight of bison grazing peacefully against the backdrop of the Mission Mountains is truly a sight to behold.

Scenic Drives: The range offers a 19-mile scenic loop that takes you through diverse landscapes, including grasslands, wetlands, and forests. Along the way, you'll have opportunities to spot bison, elk, and other wildlife.

Birdwatching: With over 200 bird species recorded, the Bison Range is a prime location for birdwatchers. Look out for bald eagles, red-tailed hawks, and various waterfowl.

Best Time to Visit

The spring and summer months are ideal for visiting the Bison Range, as wildlife is most active during these times. However, fall is also a beautiful season to visit, as the foliage changes colors and animals prepare for the colder months.

The Museum of the Rockies: A Journey Through Time

Overview: Located in Bozeman, Montana, the Museum of the Rockies is a leading natural history museum with a remarkable collection of dinosaur fossils, Native American artifacts, and exhibits on

the history of the region. The museum is home to the largest collection of dinosaur fossils in the world, making it a must-visit for history and science enthusiasts.

What to See

Dinosaur Fossils: The museum's dinosaur exhibits are world-renowned, featuring fossils from the late Cretaceous period, including a complete T. rex skeleton. The exhibits tell the story of prehistoric life and the science behind paleontological discoveries.

Native American Exhibits: The museum also showcases the history and culture of the Native American tribes of the Great Plains. Visitors can explore artifacts, clothing, and tools that provide insight into the daily lives of these cultures.

Planetarium: The museum's planetarium offers shows and exhibits that explore the night sky and the mysteries of the universe, making it an educational experience for visitors of all ages.

Historic Artifacts: The museum also features exhibits on Montana's early history, including settler artifacts, the fur trade, and the region's exploration.

Best Time to Visit

The Museum of the Rockies is open year-round, making it a great place to visit regardless of the season. The summer months may bring more visitors, but the fall and winter seasons provide a quieter, more relaxed atmosphere for exploring the exhibits at your own pace.

Montana is a state that offers diverse attractions, ranging from outdoor adventures to rich historical experiences. Whether you're hiking through glaciers, observing wildlife, skiing down snowy slopes, or exploring the past through fossils, these top attractions in Montana will provide unforgettable experiences that will stay with you long after you leave

CHAPTER 4

Hidden Gems & Unique Experiences

Montana is known for its iconic national parks like Glacier and Yellowstone, but the state also has many hidden gems that provide equally amazing experiences. These lesser-known spots offer the chance to explore quieter parts of the state, where you'll find stunning scenery, rich local culture, and fun activities. Whether you're interested in scenic drives, peaceful lakes, gemstone hunting, or lively festivals, this chapter highlights some of Montana's best-kept secrets. Get ready to discover some of the state's most special attractions!

The Beartooth Highway: Scenic Drives & Road Trips

Overview

The Beartooth Highway is one of the most beautiful and thrilling drives in the United States. This 68-mile route runs from Red Lodge to the Northeast Entrance of Yellowstone National Park, passing through the Beartooth Mountains and offering stunning views of the surrounding wilderness. The road is famous for its winding curves and high-altitude landscapes, making it one of the most dramatic and scenic highways in the country.

What to See and Do
Incredible Views: The Beartooth Highway offers breathtaking views of towering mountains, glaciers, alpine lakes, and vast valleys. As you drive through the high-altitude terrain, you'll pass snow-capped peaks and wildflower-filled meadows in summer. There are plenty of scenic overlooks where you can stop and enjoy the views.
Winding Roads: The road has many hairpin turns and switchbacks, making the drive both exciting and memorable. Whether you're driving or just enjoying the view from the passenger seat, the Beartooth Highway is an adventure in itself.
Outdoor Activities: Along the highway, you'll find many places to stop for hiking, picnicking, fishing,

or taking photos. For those looking for more adventure, consider hiking up to the Beartooth Pass or exploring the nearby Lake Plateau.

Best Time to Visit

The Beartooth Highway is usually open from mid-June to mid-September, as snow can block the road during the winter months. Summer offers the best driving conditions with clear roads and warmer weather. Early fall is also a great time to visit when the autumn foliage adds extra beauty to the drive.

Flathead Lake: Peaceful Escape

Overview: Located in the northwest corner of Montana, Flathead Lake is the largest natural freshwater lake west of the Mississippi River. It covers over 200 square miles and is known for its crystal-clear waters, scenic mountain views, and abundant outdoor activities. Flathead Lake offers a peaceful retreat where you can relax or enjoy a variety of water activities.

What to See and Do
Boating and Fishing: Flathead Lake is perfect for boating, sailing, and fishing. The lake is home to many fish species, including lake trout and yellow perch, making it a great spot for anglers.

Swimming and Picnicking: The calm waters of the lake make it ideal for swimming, especially on warm days. There are several parks and picnic areas along the shoreline where you can relax, have a meal, and enjoy the view.

Wildlife and Birdwatching: The surrounding area is full of wildlife, including bald eagles, pelicans, and osprey. Birdwatchers will enjoy spotting these birds, particularly in the quieter parts of the lake.

Lakefront Towns: Visit the charming towns around the lake, such as Polson, Bigfork, and Lakeside. These towns offer local restaurants, shopping, and opportunities for relaxing walks along the water, as well as local art galleries to explore.

Best Time to Visit

The best time to visit Flathead Lake is from June to September when the weather is warm and perfect for outdoor activities. Spring and fall are also good times to visit if you prefer a quieter, less crowded experience with pleasant temperatures for hiking and birdwatching.

Crystal Park: Gemstone Hunting

Overview: Situated in the Beaverhead-Deerlodge National Forest, Crystal Park is a hidden gem for those who enjoy hunting for gemstones. The park is well-known for its abundance of sparkling quartz crystals, and visitors can also find amethyst and calcite. Whether you're a seasoned gem hunter or a beginner, Crystal Park offers a fun and rewarding experience for everyone.

What to See and Do

Gemstone Hunting: Crystal Park's main draw is its quartz crystals. Visitors can search for these beautiful stones in the park's designated areas. The park provides tools like buckets and shovels to help you, and the staff offers advice on the best places to dig. You'll find everything from small, clear pieces to larger, dazzling formations.

Scenic Views: The park is located in a peaceful valley surrounded by mountains, offering incredible views of the surrounding wilderness. Take time to enjoy the meadows, wildflowers, and distant mountain peaks while hunting for gemstones.

Picnicking and Relaxation: After your gemstone hunt, relax with a picnic in the park. Crystal Park is an ideal spot for a family outing or a quiet retreat where you can unwind and enjoy the beauty of nature.

Best Time to Visit

The best time to visit Crystal Park is during the summer months (June to September) when the weather is ideal for outdoor activities. Spring and early fall are also good times for gemstone hunting, but winter can make conditions uncomfortable due to cold temperatures and snow.

Local Festivals and Traditions

Overview: Montana's local festivals and traditions offer a fun way to experience the state's rich culture and community spirit. From celebrating the cowboy lifestyle to honoring Native American heritage, Montana's festivals provide a lively and immersive look at the state's traditions. Whether you're enjoying music, sampling local foods, or watching a rodeo, these events are a fantastic way to connect with the heart of Montana.

Notable Festivals and Traditions

Sweet Pea Festival (Bozeman): The Sweet Pea Festival is held every summer in Bozeman and celebrates art, music, and the local community. Visitors can enjoy live performances, outdoor art shows, a lively parade, and interactive workshops. It's a great place to enjoy local culture and creativity.

Montana Folk Festival (Butte): The Montana Folk Festival, held in Butte each summer, is a three-day celebration of music, dance, and arts. It features performances by folk, blues, and roots musicians, along with crafts and local foods. The festival reflects Montana's diverse cultural backgrounds, including Native American traditions and the cowboy spirit.

Rodeo and Western Heritage Festivals: Montana is famous for its cowboy culture, and the state's rodeos showcase the thrill of bull riding, barrel racing, and calf roping. Events like the Missoula Stampede and Miles City Bucking Horse Sale highlight the skills and traditions of the rodeo.

Crow Fair (Crow Agency): The Crow Fair is one of the largest Native American celebrations in Montana. Held annually in Crow Agency, this event features powwows, parades, rodeos, and traditional Native American regalia, providing a chance to experience the beauty and culture of the Crow Nation.

Why Attend Montana's Festivals?

Authentic Experience: Attending a local festival offers a genuine glimpse into Montana's culture. These events celebrate the state's diverse traditions and are an opportunity to connect with the local community.

Community Spirit: Festivals in Montana are about more than just entertainment—they bring people together. You'll experience the warmth and friendliness of the people as you share in music, food, and festivities.

Local Cuisine: Montana's festivals often feature local food, giving you a chance to try delicious dishes like huckleberry pies, bison burgers, and hearty stews, all reflecting the state's agricultural roots.

Best Time to Visit for Festivals

Summer (June to August) is the peak festival season, with events like the Sweet Pea Festival and Montana Folk Festival. Fall is also a great time to enjoy the state's festivals, with harvest celebrations and community events in September and October.

Montana's hidden gems and unique experiences provide a chance to explore the state in a more personal way. Whether you're driving along the Beartooth Highway, relaxing by Flathead Lake, searching for gemstones at Crystal Park, or immersing yourself in the local culture at a festival, these attractions offer a deeper connection to Montana's natural beauty and vibrant traditions. These experiences will add unforgettable memories to your Montana adventure.

CHAPTER 5

Outdoor Adventures

Montana is a dream destination for outdoor lovers. With its vast landscapes, towering mountains, clear lakes, and open spaces, the state provides a wide range of outdoor activities that allow you to connect with nature. Whether you're looking for a challenge or just want to enjoy the beauty of the landscape, Montana has something for everyone. This chapter highlights some of the best outdoor activities in the state, including hiking, wildlife watching, water sports, winter sports, and scenic drives. So grab your gear—Montana's outdoor adventures are ready for you!

Hiking and Trekking: Trails in Glacier & Yellowstone

Montana offers some of the best hiking trails in the country, with spots like Glacier National Park and Yellowstone providing incredible scenery. Whether you want a tough climb or a simple walk in nature, Montana's trails cater to all levels of hikers.

What to See and Do

Glacier National Park

Highline Trail: This challenging 11.8-mile trail offers amazing views along the Continental Divide, with stunning views of peaks, valleys, and glaciers. It's a tough hike with steep drops, but the views are worth the effort.

Grinnell Glacier Trail: A 7.6-mile trail that takes you to Grinnell Glacier, passing clear lakes, waterfalls, and meadows. It's a moderately difficult hike with amazing views of the glacier.

Hidden Lake Overlook: A shorter, 3-mile hike offering beautiful views of Hidden Lake and nearby mountains. It's perfect for those looking for a scenic adventure without too much effort.

Yellowstone National Park

Lone Star Geyser Trail: A 2.5-mile trail leading to the Lone Star Geyser, where you can watch it erupt. It's an easy hike, making it a great choice for families.

Mount Washburn Trail: A 6-mile trail that climbs to the top of Mount Washburn, offering panoramic views of Yellowstone's landscape. The summit offers sweeping views of geysers, lakes, and forests.

Uncle Tom's Trail: A short but steep trail (about 0.25 miles) that takes you down into Yellowstone Canyon with stunning views of the Lower Falls.

Best Time to Visit

The best time for hiking in Montana is from June to September, when most trails are open and accessible. Early summer offers wildflowers, and fall brings beautiful foliage. However, be prepared for sudden weather changes, especially at higher altitudes.

Wildlife Safaris and Birdwatching in Montana

Montana's wide range of habitats, from forests to wetlands and grasslands, makes it a prime destination for wildlife lovers. The state is home to a variety of animals, including grizzly bears, bison, elk, and hundreds of bird species. Whether you're a photographer or just someone who enjoys observing nature, Montana is the place to be.

What to See and Do

Grizzly Bears and Bison in Yellowstone: Yellowstone is one of the best places to spot grizzly bears, bison, wolves, and elk, especially in the Lamar and Hayden Valleys. Early mornings and evenings are the best times for wildlife sightings.

Bison and Elk at the National Bison Range: The National Bison Range, located in northwestern Montana, is home to a large bison herd, as well as elk, deer, and other wildlife. The 19-mile scenic drive gives you plenty of chances to spot these animals in their natural environment.

Birdwatching at Flathead Lake: Flathead Lake is great for birdwatching, with over 200 bird species, including bald eagles, osprey, and pelicans. The surrounding wetlands and forests also attract migratory birds.

Best Time to Visit

The best time for wildlife watching in Montana is from spring to fall when animals are most active.

While winter offers a quieter experience, it can be harder to spot some species.

Water Activities: Kayaking, Boating, and Fishing

Overview: Montana is home to many pristine lakes, rivers, and reservoirs that are perfect for water activities. Whether you love kayaking, fishing, or boating, the state offers endless opportunities to enjoy its beautiful waters.

What to See and Do

Kayaking on Flathead Lake: Flathead Lake is ideal for kayaking, with clear waters and breathtaking views of the surrounding mountains. Rent a kayak or canoe and explore the lake's serene environment.

Boating on the Missouri River: The Missouri

River offers plenty of room for powerboating, sailing, and relaxing cruises. It's one of the longest rivers in North America and a great place for water lovers.

Fishing in the Yellowstone River: The Yellowstone River is perfect for fishing, with opportunities to catch trout, bass, and walleye. Fly fishing is especially popular here, and many anglers visit in spring and fall for the best fishing conditions.

Best Time to Visit

Summer is the peak season for water activities, from June to September, when the weather is warm and the waters are calm. However, spring and fall offer a quieter experience, with mild temperatures and excellent fishing.

Winter Sports: Skiing, Snowboarding, and Snowshoeing

Overview: Montana's winters are known for their excellent skiing and snowboarding. With resorts like Big Sky, Whitefish, and Bridger Bowl, the state offers slopes for all levels, along with snowshoeing, cross-country skiing, and ice fishing. Whether you're into fast-paced mountain sports or peaceful snowshoe hikes, Montana's winter sports scene has something for everyone.

What to See and Do

Big Sky Resort: Big Sky Resort is one of the largest ski areas in the U.S., with over 5,800 acres of terrain. The resort has slopes for all skill levels, along with terrain parks, tree runs, and backcountry areas.

Whitefish Mountain Resort: Whitefish Mountain Resort is another great spot for skiing and snowboarding, with beautiful views of Whitefish Lake. The resort also offers tubing, snowshoeing, and ice skating.

Snowshoeing in Glacier National Park: Glacier National Park offers several snowshoeing trails, providing a peaceful way to explore the park's winter landscape.

Best Time to Visit

The best time for winter sports in Montana is from December to March, when snowfall is abundant, and ski resorts are in full swing. Spring (March and April) also offers great skiing with warmer temperatures and longer days

Scenic Drives: Exploring Montana's Natural Beauty

Overview

Montana is home to some of the most scenic drives in the U.S., with winding roads that pass through forests, mountains, and plains. These drives let you take in the state's stunning landscapes at your own pace, with plenty of stops for hiking, sightseeing, and wildlife watching.

What to See and Do

Going-to-the-Sun Road: This 50-mile road in Glacier National Park is one of the most famous scenic drives, crossing the Continental Divide and offering views of the park's rugged beauty.

Beartooth Highway: The Beartooth Highway is a 68-mile stretch of road from Red Lodge to Yellowstone, offering views of glaciers, mountain peaks, and alpine lakes.

Flathead Lake Scenic Drive: This 30-mile drive takes you along the shores of Flathead Lake, offering beautiful views of the lake, the Mission Mountains, and the surrounding forests.

Best Time to Visit

Scenic drives are best enjoyed in summer and fall, when the weather is clear, and the roads are open. Early fall also offers the beauty of autumn foliage, making it one of the best times for a drive through Montana's landscapes.

Montana offers outdoor adventures for all kinds of explorers, whether you're hiking through the national parks, watching wildlife, enjoying water sports, skiing in the winter, or taking in the scenery on a scenic drive. The state is packed with natural beauty and exciting activities that will make your Montana adventure unforgettable.

Pictograph Cave State Park

Chapter 6

Food and Drink

Montana offers a culinary experience as diverse and rich as its landscapes. Whether you're craving a classic steakhouse meal, a refreshing craft beer, or an upscale dining experience, the state has something for everyone. From hearty Western dishes to locally sourced, seasonal specialties, you'll find a variety of delicious options to satisfy your taste. This chapter will take you through Montana's top food and drink experiences, including local cuisine, the best places to eat, and the craft beer and spirits scene. Whether you're a foodie or just someone looking to enjoy a meal in a unique setting, Montana has plenty to offer

Classic Montana Cuisine: Steaks, Bison, and More

Jake's Downtown

Jake's Downtown is a locally owned steakhouse, established in 1979, located in the Historic Grand Building. It features two bars and offers both casual and fine dining. With strong ties to the community, we are proud to contribute to the continued growth of Downtown Billings for the next 40 years

Hours: Monday to Friday -11:00 AM - 5:00 PM

Saturday - 5:00 PM - 10:00 PM

Price: $30 - $50 per person

Address: 2701 1st Ave N, Billings, MT 59101-2308

Website: jakesdt.**com**

Tamarack Brewing Company

Tamarack Brewing Company, located in the heart of Missoula, offers a great mix of traditional Montana dishes, focusing on hearty steaks, tasty bison meals, and a variety of local beers. This popular brewery and restaurant serves a wide range of dishes that highlight the region's rich flavors, including juicy steaks and bison burgers, all made with fresh, locally sourced ingredients. Whether you're in the mood for a delicious meal with a cold craft beer or simply want to relax in a comfortable setting, Tamarack Brewing Company offers a true Montana dining experience.

Price: $20-$40 per person

Address: 231 W Front St, Missoula, MT 59802-4301

Hours: Monday - Friday: 11:00 AM - 9:00 PM

Saturday: 10:00 AM - 10:00 PM

Sunday: 10:00 AM - 9:00 PM

Website: tamarackbrewing.com

The Montana Club (Helena)

Overview: The Montana Club Restaurant offers a wide variety of dishes, including steakhouse steaks, seafood, sandwiches, burgers, pasta, salads, and more. While dining, enjoy a seasonal microbrew, wine, or a perfectly crafted cocktail in the Montana Club lounge. They also offer a daily Happy Hour from 3:00 to 5:30 PM with Buy One, Get One drinks! With locations in Missoula, Butte, Great Falls, Billings, and Kalispell, it's Montana's top hometown restaurant.

Hours: Monday to Friday, 11:00 AM - 9:00 PM

Address: 4561 N Reserve St, Missoula, MT 59808-1410

Website: montanaclub.com

Best Places to Eat in Montana: From Fine Dining to Local Delights

Montana Ale Works

Overview: Located in Bozeman, Montana Ale Works offers delicious food and a wide range of local craft beers. The restaurant features a variety of dishes, from gourmet burgers and seafood to comfort foods, all made with fresh, local ingredients. With a lively atmosphere and modern-rustic decor, it's a popular spot for both locals and visitors. Whether you're enjoying a meal or grabbing a drink, Montana Ale Works is a great place to experience Montana's culinary scene.

Hours: Monday - Sunday - 4:00PM - 9:00PM

Price: $20 - $40 per person

Address: 611 E Main St, Bozeman, MT 59715-3778

Website: montanaaleworks.com

The Bistro at the Billings Depot (Billings)

Overview: Located in the historic Billings Depot, The Bistro offers a blend of local and contemporary dishes in a charming setting. With a focus on seasonal ingredients and locally sourced meats, the restaurant provides a great dining experience.

Hours: Monday- Friday- 9:00AM - 4:00PM

Address: 2310 Montana Ave, Billings, MT 59101

Website: bistroatthebillingsdepot.com

Café Zydeco (Bozeman)

Overview: Café Zydeco brings the flavors of Louisiana to Montana, serving up Cajun and Creole-inspired dishes like gumbo, jambalaya, and po'boys. This lively, casual eatery offers a fun, flavorful dining experience in the heart of Bozeman.

Price: $10 - $30 per person

Hours: Monday - 11:00AM - 2:00PM

Tuesday - Saturday - 11:00AM - 3:00PM

Sunday - 10- 2:00PM

Address: 312 N 1st Ave, Bozeman, MT 59715

Website: zydecobozeman.com

Craft Breweries and Distilleries

Big Sky Brewing Co. (Missoula)

Overview: Big Sky Brewing Co. is one of Montana's most popular craft breweries, known for its signature Moose Drool Brown Ale and seasonal brews. Visitors can enjoy tasting sessions and brewery tours while relaxing in a laid-back setting.

Hours: Monday - Saturday - 11:00AM - 8:00PM

Sunday - 12:00PM - 6:00

Address: 5417 Trumpeter Way, Missoula, MT 59808

Website: bigskybrew.

Willie's Distillery (Ennis)

Overview: Willie's Distillery produces small-batch spirits, including whiskey, gin, and vodka, all made from Montana-grown grains. As a family-owned business, it offers a true taste of the state's distilling heritage, with tours and tastings available for visitors:

Address: 312 Main St, Ennis, MT 59729, United States

Website: williesdistillery.com

Dry Hills Distillery (Missoula)

Overview: Known for its high-quality vodka and gin made from local Montana grains, Dry Hills Distillery provides a great opportunity to learn about the distillation process and enjoy some tastings of their handcrafted spirits.

Hours: Monday -Friday 2:00pm - 8:00pm

Saturday - 12:00pm - 8:00pm

Address: 106 Village Center Lane, Bozeman, MT 59718, United States

Website: dryhillsdistillery.com

Montana's food and drink scene offers something for every palate, from classic Montana cuisine featuring steaks and bison to refined fine dining and refreshing craft beers. Whether you're dining at a cozy café or sipping a locally crafted spirit, the state's culinary delights will make your visit even more memorable.

CHAPTER 7

Accommodation Options

Montana provides a wide variety of places to stay, making it easy to find accommodations that match your budget and travel style. Whether you're looking for a luxurious resort with stunning views, a comfortable hotel for a relaxing stay, an affordable motel, or a one-of-a-kind experience like glamping or a stay at a dude ranch, Montana has options for every type of traveler. In this chapter, we'll look at some of the best choices, with information on prices, locations, and websites for your convenience.

Luxury Hotels and Resorts in Montana

The Resort at Paws Up (Greenough)

Overview: Set in a beautiful wilderness location, The Resort at Paws Up combines luxury and adventure. With glamping tents, private homes, and ranch cabins, it's perfect for those looking to enjoy both comfort and outdoor activities like horseback riding and fly fishing. The resort also offers a world-class spa

Price: $2,500 to $3,000 per night, depending on accommodation and season.

Address: 40060 Paws Up Rd, Greenough, MT 59823
Website: pawsup.com

The Fairmont Hot Springs Resort (Fairmont)

Overview: Situated in the scenic Bitterroot Valley, this resort is known for its hot springs pools and full-service spa. Guests can enjoy spacious rooms, an 18-hole golf course, and nearby hiking and skiing.

Price: $150 to $400 per night.

Address: 1500 Fairmont Rd, Fairmont, MT 59711

Website: fairmont.com

The Lodge at Whitefish Lake (Whitefish)

Overview: This luxurious resort on the shores of Whitefish Lake offers a stunning lakeside view, private marina, spa services, and fine dining. It's a great choice for those who want to enjoy Montana's beauty in a high-end setting.

Price: $250 to $300 per night.

Address: 1380 Wisconsin Ave, Whitefish, MT 59937

Website: lodgeatwhitefishlake.com

Mid-Range Stays: Comfortable and Convenient

The Best Western Plus Grant Creek Inn (Missoula)

Overview: This comfortable hotel is located just a short drive from downtown Missoula. It offers all the amenities you need for a pleasant stay, including easy access to shopping, dining, and outdoor activities.

Price: $250 to $300 per night.

Address: 5280 Grant Creek Rd, Missoula, MT 59808

Website: bestwestern.com

Holiday Inn Missoula Downtown (Missoula)

Overview: A modern hotel with comfortable rooms, an indoor pool, fitness center, and on-site restaurant, located in the heart of downtown Missoula. It's perfect for visitors wanting to be close to local attractions like the University of Montana.

Price: $250 to $300 per night.

Address: 200 S Pattee St, Missoula, MT 59802

Website: ihg.com

The Polson Inn (Polson)

Overview: Near Flathead Lake, this cozy inn offers easy access to local attractions like the lake and Glacier National Park. It's ideal for families or solo travelers looking for a comfortable and convenient stay.

Price: $80 to $150 per night.

Address: 402 1st St E, Polson, MT 59860

Website: polsoninn.com

Budget-Friendly Lodging: Motels, Hostels, and Campsites

Super 8 by Wyndham Missoula/Reserve Street (Missoula)

Overview: This affordable motel provides basic amenities, including free breakfast and Wi-Fi. Conveniently located near Interstate 90, it's a good option for travelers passing through or exploring the area.

Price: $70 to $120 per night.
Address: 4703 N Reserve St, Missoula, MT 59808, United States
Website: wyndhamhotels.com

Homewood Suites by Hilton Bozeman

Overview: Homewood Suites by Hilton Bozeman offers affordable and comfortable accommodations with spacious rooms and fully equipped kitchens, making it ideal for long stays or guests who want a home-like experience. The hotel provides amenities such as free breakfast, an indoor pool, a fitness center, and a social evening reception. It's located near downtown Bozeman, giving easy access to local attractions, making it great for both business and leisure travelers.

Price: $130 to $160

Address: 1023 Baxter Ln, Bozeman, MT 59715
Website: hilton.com

Lolo Creek Campground (Lolo)

Overview: For those who want to camp, Lolo Creek Campground offers a budget-friendly experience surrounded by nature, with access to Lolo National Forest for hiking and wildlife watching.

Price: $15 to $30 per night.

Address: Lolo National Forest, Forest Road #2170, Lolo, MT 59847, United States

Website: campendium.com

Unique Accommodations: Dude Ranches, Cabins, and Glamping

The Ranch at Rock Creek (Philipsburg)

Overview: A luxury dude ranch offering an all-inclusive experience with activities like horseback riding and fishing. It's a great place for adventure and relaxation in Montana's wilderness.

Price: Starting at $,2,500 per night for all-inclusive accommodations.
Address: 1230 Burnt Fork Rd, Philipsburg, MT 59858
Website: theranchatrockcreek.com

Glacier Under Canvas (Coram)

Overview: For a luxurious camping experience, Glacier Under Canvas offers safari-style tents with king-sized beds and private bathrooms. Located near Glacier National Park, it combines the thrill of the outdoors with modern comfort.

Price: $250 to $600 per night, depending on the season and tent type.
Address: 101 Under Canvas Rd, Coram, MT 59913, United States
Website: undercanvas.com

Montana has an accommodation option for everyone, from luxurious resorts to budget-friendly motels and unique stays like dude ranches and glamping sites. Whether you're looking for a relaxing retreat or an adventurous experience, these diverse lodging options ensure your stay in the state is comfortable and memorable.

CHAPTER 8

Day Trips and Excursions

Montana's diverse landscapes make it an ideal destination for day trips and adventures. If you're staying in one of the state's charming cities, you're just a short drive away from a range of scenic spots and exciting activities. Whether you're interested in breathtaking mountain views, picturesque valleys, or quaint small towns, Montana has something to offer. In this chapter, we'll look at some of the best day trips from Billings, Missoula, and Bozeman, along with the beauty of Flathead Valley, the Mission Mountains, and the Bitterroot Valley.

Day Trips from Billings, Missoula, and Bozeman

Montana's major cities are perfect starting points for memorable day trips. Here are some great excursions to explore from Billings, Missoula, and Bozeman.

Billings:

Pictograph Cave State Park (30 miles south)

Just outside Billings, Pictograph Cave State Park offers a fascinating look at ancient Native American rock art. The park features three caves with drawings over 2,000 years old. Visitors can hike the scenic trails to the caves and enjoy views of the Yellowstone Valley. It's a great spot for history lovers and outdoor enthusiasts.

Yellowstone River and Pompeys Pillar (50 miles southeast)

A short drive from Billings, the Yellowstone River is perfect for a relaxing getaway. Pompeys Pillar National Monument is a historical site where Captain William Clark carved his name in 1806. A short hike to the top of the sandstone pillar provides stunning views of the area. It's ideal for hiking, photography, and learning about early American exploration

Missoula:

Lolo National Forest (20 miles southwest)

Lolo National Forest is just a short drive from Missoula, offering a wide range of outdoor activities like hiking, fishing, and wildlife watching. The forest's diverse landscapes, from lush woods to rugged mountains, provide plenty of opportunities to enjoy nature.

Kootenai Creek and the Rattlesnake Wilderness (30 miles north)

North of Missoula, the Rattlesnake Wilderness is known for its beautiful alpine scenery. The Kootenai Creek trailhead offers an easy-to-moderate hike that leads to a peaceful mountain lake surrounded by towering peaks.

Bozeman:

Big Sky Resort and the Gallatin Canyon (45 miles south)

Big Sky Resort is perfect for a day trip any time of year. It offers skiing in the winter and hiking, mountain biking, and zip-lining in the summer. The Gallatin Canyon provides stunning views and great outdoor opportunities.

Museum of the Rockies and Hyalite Canyon (15 miles south)

The Museum of the Rockies in Bozeman is famous for its dinosaur fossils. After visiting the museum, head to nearby Hyalite Canyon for hiking, fishing, or picnicking. In winter, it's a great place for snowshoeing and ice climbing.

Flathead Valley and the Mission Mountains

Located in northwestern Montana, Flathead Valley is famous for its natural beauty, including Flathead Lake, one of the largest freshwater lakes in the U.S. The valley is surrounded by the majestic Mission Mountains to the east and the Swan Mountains to the west. Here's a look at some of the area's highlights:

Flathead Lake

Flathead Lake is perfect for a day of water activities like kayaking, boating, and fishing. You can rent kayaks or paddleboards to explore the clear waters, or take a boat tour to enjoy the views of the surrounding mountains. Several state parks along the lake, such as West Shore State Park and Big Arm State Park, offer picnic areas and hiking trails.

The Mission Mountains

The Mission Mountains offer a rugged wilderness ideal for hiking and wildlife watching. The Jewel Basin Hiking Area features stunning trails that lead to alpine lakes with breathtaking views of the valley. It's perfect for those looking for a day of adventure and natural beauty.

Polson and Bigfork

Polson and Bigfork are charming towns along Flathead Lake. Polson is known for the Flathead Lake Cherry Festival, while Bigfork is home to art galleries and boutique shops. Both towns are great places to relax, enjoy local food, and take in the lakefront scenery.

Exploring the Bitterroot Valley

The Bitterroot Valley, in southwestern Montana, is a hidden gem for outdoor enthusiasts, history lovers, and those seeking small-town charm. The valley is surrounded by the Bitterroot Mountains to the west and the Sapphire Mountains to the east. Here are a few places to explore:

Hamilton and the Bitterroot National Forest

Hamilton is the heart of the Bitterroot Valley and a gateway to the Bitterroot National Forest. The forest offers numerous hiking trails, campgrounds, and opportunities for wildlife viewing. Whether you're fishing in the rivers or exploring mountain lakes, the Bitterroot National Forest is full of natural beauty.

Stevensville and Fort Owen State Park

Stevensville, Montana's first permanent settlementis a historic town worth visiting. Fort Owen State Park, located here, preserves the site of one of Montana's first military outposts. The park offers peaceful walking trails and scenic views of the Bitterroot Mountains, making it a relaxing stop.

Lake Como and the Sapphire Mountains

Lake Como, tucked away in the Sapphire Mountains, is a peaceful retreat for fishing, kayaking, and picnicking. The surrounding trails offer a chance to explore the forest and nearby peaks, making Lake Como a great place for nature lovers to unwind.

Montana offers a wide range of day trips and excursions for those eager to explore the state's natural wonders. Whether you're hiking in the mountains, relaxing by the lake, or visiting historic sites, these trips allow you to experience the best of what Montana has to offer.

CHAPTER 9

Health and Safety Tips

When planning your trip to Montana, it's essential to stay informed about health and safety precautions to ensure you have a safe and enjoyable adventure. With its vast wilderness, wildlife, and unpredictable weather, you need to be ready for different situations. This chapter will provide you with important health and safety tips, how to handle wildlife encounters, and where to find emergency services in Montana. By following these tips, you'll be well-prepared to explore the state safely.

Health and Safety Tips for Your Montana Adventure

Montana offers a variety of outdoor activities such as hiking, skiing, fishing, and camping, often in remote areas where medical help could be far away. Being prepared is key to ensuring a safe trip. Here are a few tips to keep in mind:

Stay Hydrated: Montana's dry climate can quickly lead to dehydration, especially in the summer. Always carry plenty of water during outdoor activities, especially if you're in higher elevations where dehydration can occur more easily. Drink often, even if you're not thirsty.

Protect Yourself from the Sun: Montana's high elevation means you're closer to the sun, so you can burn more easily. Use sunscreen with high SPF on exposed skin, and wear a hat and sunglasses. Reapply sunscreen after swimming or sweating.

Prepare for Changing Weather: Montana's weather can change quickly, especially in the mountains. Even in summer, temperatures can drop unexpectedly. Always bring layers of clothing you can add or remove and pack a lightweight waterproof jacket.

Altitude Awareness: Many outdoor activities in Montana, such as hiking in Glacier National Park, take place at high altitudes. If you're not used to high altitudes, take it easy at first. Symptoms of altitude sickness include headaches, dizziness, and shortness of breath. Drink plenty of water, avoid alcohol, and take breaks to adjust.

Pack a First Aid Kit: If you're hiking or camping in remote areas, bring a basic first aid kit. Include bandages, antiseptic wipes, blister treatment, pain relievers, tweezers (for splinters), and any personal medications. Also, consider packing specific supplies depending on the activities you'll be doing, like a snake bite kit if you plan on hiking in areas where snakes are common.

Check for Ticks: Montana has ticks that can spread diseases like Lyme disease. After outdoor activities, check yourself, your children, and pets for ticks. Wear long sleeves and pants and use insect repellent to reduce the risk.

Dealing with Wildlife Encounters

Montana is home to a variety of wildlife, including bison, elk, and potentially dangerous animals like bears and mountain lions. Knowing how to safely handle these encounters is crucial. Here's what to do:

Bear Safety: Montana has both grizzly and black bears, and you may come across them, especially in national parks like Glacier and Yellowstone. Follow these tips:

Make noise while hiking to alert bears of your presence. Bears are less likely to approach if they hear you coming.

Carry bear spray and know how to use it. Bear spray is the best defense against bear attacks.

Never approach a bear and avoid running if you encounter one, as it may trigger a chase.

Store food and scented items in bear-proof containers or hang them high and far from your campsite.

Dealing with Bison and Other Large Animals: Bison can weigh over 2,000 pounds and can be dangerous. Keep at least 100 yards away from bison. Always stay in your vehicle or keep at least 50 feet distance when taking photos. Be cautious with elk, moose, and deer, especially during their rutting season in the fall.

Mountain Lion Safety: Mountain lions tend to avoid humans, but if you do encounter one, stay calm and make yourself appear larger. Do not run, as it may provoke the lion. If attacked, defend yourself with anything you have, such as a stick, bear spray, or rocks.

Avoiding Snakes: Montana has a few species of snakes, including rattlesnakes. To avoid snake bites:

Stick to clear paths and avoid tall grass or brush.

Be mindful of where you step and where you place your hands when climbing or reaching.

If you see a snake, slowly back away. Don't try to handle or capture it.

First Aid & Emergency Services in Montana

While Montana's outdoor activities can be exciting, accidents can happen. It's important to know where to get help if needed:

Emergency Contacts:
911 is the universal emergency number in Montana. Use it for medical emergencies, fires, or any dangerous situation.

In remote areas, cell phone service may be limited. It's a good idea to tell someone your plans and expected return time. If you're going to places with no cell service, consider bringing a satellite phone or personal locator beacon.

Hospitals and Clinics: While Montana has several hospitals and urgent care clinics, they might be spread out in rural areas. Larger cities like Billings, Missoula, and Bozeman have easy access to medical facilities, but if you're heading into rural areas, check the nearest hospital before leaving.

Search and Rescue: If you get lost or hurt in remote areas, Montana has a well-established search and rescue network. Use any communication devices you have to call for help, and many hiking areas and national parks provide instructions on how to contact rescue teams.

Medical Supplies: In addition to a first aid kit, consider bringing medication for allergies or pain, and any other medical supplies you may need. It's also helpful to have an emergency whistle, headlamp, and space blanket in case of sudden weather changes or accidents.

Wildfire Safety: Montana's summer months can bring the risk of wildfires, especially in dry areas. If you're camping, make sure to fully extinguish your campfire before leaving or going to sleep. Stay informed about fire warnings and be ready to evacuate if necessary.

By following these health and safety tips, being cautious around wildlife, and knowing where to seek help, you'll ensure a safe and enjoyable Montana adventure. Be prepared, respect the environment, and enjoy the incredible beauty and excitement this state has to offer.

CHAPTER 10

Bonus Section

Itineraries

7-Day Montana Itinerary: Nature, Culture, and Adventure

Montana is a fantastic blend of outdoor activities, rich culture, and stunning landscapes. Whether you're seeking adventure in nature or a peaceful retreat, this 7-day itinerary will guide you to the best experiences in the state, from breathtaking national parks to charming towns and local gems.

Day 1: Arrival in Bozeman & Town Exploration

Morning:
Arrive in Bozeman, a vibrant town with a lot to offer. Start your day at Montana Ale Works for a hearty breakfast and a local craft beer in a cozy setting.

Afternoon:
Visit the Museum of the Rockies, which showcases impressive dinosaur fossils and exhibits about Montana's history. Take a leisurely stroll through downtown Bozeman, exploring local shops, cafés, and art galleries.

Evening:
For dinner, head to Jake's Downtown for a tasty steak and classic Montana cuisine.

Overnight: Stay in Bozeman at Homewood Suites by Hilton Bozeman for a comfortable night.

Day 2: Big Sky Resort & Gallatin Canyon Adventure

Morning:
Drive 45 minutes to Big Sky Resort in Gallatin

Canyon for a day of outdoor fun. In the summer, enjoy hiking, mountain biking, and scenic gondola rides with incredible mountain views.

Afternoon:
After lunch at the resort, head to Hyalite Canyon for a peaceful hike or a picnic by the lake. If you're visiting in winter, enjoy snowshoeing or ice climbing.

Evening:
Return to Bozeman and unwind with a meal at The Red Bird, known for its farm-to-table dishes.

Overnight: Stay in Bozeman for the night.

Day 3: Drive to Missoula & Lolo National Forest

Morning:
Drive to Missoula, a charming college town. After breakfast at a local café, explore Lolo National Forest, just 20 miles southwest. This forest offers a variety of trails, perfect for hiking, fishing, or wildlife watching.

Afternoon:
For lunch, visit Tamarack Brewing Company for bison steaks and locally brewed beers. Explore

Missoula's downtown, with its art galleries, shops, and museums.

Evening:
For dinner, enjoy casual dining at Café Zydeco, offering delicious Cajun and Creole dishes.

Overnight: Stay in Missoula for the night.

Day 4: Pictograph Cave State Park & Billings

Morning:
Drive to Billings, Montana's largest city. Stop at Pictograph Cave State Park on the way to explore ancient Native American rock art and enjoy stunning views of the Yellowstone Valley.

Afternoon:
In Billings, have lunch at The Montana Club, known for its great steaks. Then visit Pompeys Pillar National Monument, where Captain William Clark carved his name during the Lewis and Clark Expedition.

Evening:
For dinner, enjoy traditional Montana comfort food at The Stockyard Café.

Overnight: Stay in Billings.

Day 5: Yellowstone National Park Exploration

Morning:

Drive to Yellowstone National Park to explore its famous geothermal features like Old Faithful and Grand Prismatic Spring. Capture the vibrant colors and unique wonders of the park.

Afternoon:

Spot wildlife in Hayden Valley and Lamar Valley, where you might see bison, elk, and wolves. Take time for a short hike or a picnic to immerse yourself in Yellowstone's beauty.

Evening:

Return to your accommodations or stay within the park for a relaxing evening.

Overnight: Stay at one of the park's lodges or campgrounds.

Day 6: Glacier National Park Adventure

Morning:

Travel north to Glacier National Park and hike Going-to-the-Sun Road, which offers breathtaking views of glaciers, waterfalls, and valleys.

Afternoon:
Visit Lake McDonald for a boat ride or swim, and hike the Hidden Lake Overlook trail for amazing views. Explore the area's wildlife and natural beauty.

Evening:
For dinner, relax with a meal at a local restaurant near the park.

Overnight: Stay near Glacier National Park.

Day 7: Flathead Lake & Mission Mountains

Morning:
Drive through Flathead Valley and visit Flathead Lake, one of the largest freshwater lakes in the U.S. Enjoy kayaking or paddleboarding on the lake, or have a picnic at one of the nearby parks.

Afternoon:
Explore the Mission Mountains, which offer rugged trails leading to alpine lakes. If you prefer a slower pace, visit Polson or Bigfork for a charming lunch and shopping.

Evening:
Finish your trip with a relaxing dinner in Bigfork, known for its artsy atmosphere and lakeside dining.

Overnight: Return to Kalispell or Bozeman for your departure.

Final Thoughts

This 7-day itinerary ensures you experience Montana's natural beauty, outdoor adventures, rich history, and local culture. From iconic national parks to hidden gems, you'll leave with unforgettable memories of this stunning state.

CONCLUSION

Montana, often called the "Treasure State," truly lives up to its name by offering a wide range of experiences for all kinds of travelers. From towering mountains and crystal-clear lakes to charming towns and fascinating history, Montana combines natural beauty and human spirit in unforgettable ways. Whether you're hiking through the rugged terrain of Glacier National Park, watching wildlife in Yellowstone, or relaxing by the peaceful waters of Flathead Lake, every part of this state has something unique to offer.

This book has given you a taste of what Montana holds, from outdoor adventures to its rich cultural heritage and delicious local food. But beyond these pages, Montana invites you to explore on your own, discover hidden gems, and embrace the stunning landscapes and lively communities that make this state so special.

So, pack your bags, put on your hiking boots, and begin your journey. Montana is waiting for you with wide-open skies, breathtaking views, and experiences that will stay with you long after you leave. Whether you crave adventure or seek quiet moments in nature, Montana offers memories that will last forever.

The Treasure State is more than just a place—it's an adventure, a journey, and an invitation to explore the magic of the American West. So, go ahead, embrace the spirit of Montana, and create your own unforgettable experience here.

Printed in Dunstable, United Kingdom